BRITAIN'S HERITAGE

Tea Gardens

Twigs Way

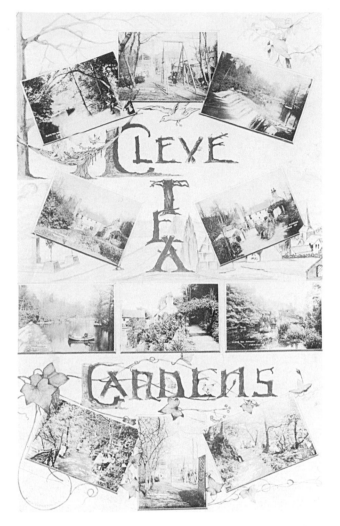

A rare advertising postcard depicting a variety of views of the popular Cleeve Tea Gardens.

First published 2017

Amberley Publishing
The Hill, Stroud
Gloucestershire, GL5 4EP

www.amberley-books.com

Copyright © Twigs Way, 2017

The right of Twigs Way to be identified as the Author of this work has been asserted in accordance with the Copyrights, Designs and Patents Act 1988.

ISBN 978 1 4456 7001 0 (paperback)
ISBN 978 1 4456 7002 7 (ebook)

British Library Cataloguing in Publication Data.
A catalogue record for this book is available from the British Library.

Printed in the UK.

Contents

1
Anyone for Tea?

Visions of orchards in blossom, rustic tables, colourful deckchairs, silver teapots and mismatched china: the tea garden brings together two of the most quintessentially British activities. Spanning the period from the eighteenth century to the mid-twentieth, the tea garden is experiencing a revival in an age when simple delights entice us once again. Every summer new tea gardens arrive and old ones re-open, while indoor tea rooms sprout outdoor tables and bright flower borders. But what is the history of the tea garden, and how does it differ from its racier cousins the coffee house, the beer garden or the spa? When did tea gardens first appear, who did they appeal to, and indeed how does one define a 'tea garden'? The traditional English tea garden was usually a relatively small one, perhaps a welcoming cottage garden adapted for passing travellers, walkers and cyclists. Sometimes situated overlooking well-known beauty spots, alongside rivers, or (after the advent of the car) on windy hilltops, the location was predominantly rural, although large urban parks in London and other cities sometimes boasted seating around a tea pavilion or bandstand. Owing little in aesthetic influence to the original tea-growing countries, they rarely encompassed the Chinese or Japanese themes of the American tea garden but instead encourage the mythology of the unique Britishness of tea drinking.

Deckchairs and tables under fruit trees is the most traditional tea garden layout, as seen here at the Orchard Tea Garden in Grantchester. (Courtesy of The Orchard Tea Garden)

'Rustic' became the traditional style for tea gardens in the Victorian and Edwardian periods.

Tea was not introduced to England until the seventeenth century. Infusing and drinking the leaves of the shrub *Camellia sinensis* was supposedly first discovered by the mythical Chinese Emperor Shen Nung, in 2,737 BC, when the leaves from a nearby bush blew into his pot of boiling water, and it would be nice to think that he was sitting in a garden when this happened. By the twelfth century tea was being traded and drunk across China, Tibet, Nepal, India and the Middle East. Thanks to the trading companies of the Dutch and Portuguese, tea made its way to mainland Europe from about 1610, with the first shipment to England said to date to 1657.

Did you know?

Catherine of Braganza was said to have brought a casket of tea with her from Portugal when she married Charles II in 1662. King Charles himself would also have encountered tea during his exile in The Hague, where early tea gardens made their first appearance.

Initially tea was consumed in the relatively new but increasingly popular coffee houses, alongside chocolate, brandy and the more traditional ales and strong wines. Coffee houses were almost exclusively male establishments, where news and politics were discussed in an atmosphere made heavy with smoke from tobacco pipes. Both tea and coffee were heated continuously on smoky hearths, and served sweetened but without milk, resulting in a strong viscous liquid unlike the delicate flavouring of the Chinese Emperor's accidental leaves.

The tea plant is a native of China and tea was not available in Europe until the seventeenth century.

In 1658 the variously named 'Tcha', 'Tay' or 'Tea' was advertised in the periodical *Mercurius Politicus* as being sold at the Sultaness-head, a famous coffee house in London, and the diarist Samuel Pepys recorded drinking 'tee' for the first time two years later. Between 1669 and 1678 the volume of tea imports increased almost forty-fold in England, from 143 lbs to 5,000 lbs, as the fashion for tea drinking spread among the court and the aristocracy.

Respectable women did not frequent coffee houses and so loose-leafed tea was also sold from the coffee house counter for home consumption. Upper-class women would gather with their friends for elaborate tea parties in their private sitting rooms or dressing rooms, and tea wares proliferated in response to these. Small delicate bowls and matching saucers came from China along with the tea itself, acting as heavy ballast for the ships. Teaspoons, teapots, and the apparatus for heating water all appeared and would later reappear in the paraphernalia of the tea garden, although English silver teapots competed with the China teapot in aristocratic households. Entire rooms were set aside for the taking of tea in wealthier households and were decorated to echo the exotic origins of the tea itself. At Claydon House in Buckinghamshire a 'tea alcove' was installed in the Chinese Room in appropriately Chinoiserie style with two small figures on either side. Out-of-doors tea houses, often in the same Chinese style, were also installed in many eighteenth-century gardens and were again associated particularly with ladies' tea parties. In 1772, Mary Jemima Yorke recorded that at Wrest Park (Bedfordshire) the house party took tea in the 'Pavilion' on Saturday evening, trying the echo out of doors and listening to Lady Montfort sing French songs. The building still survives at Wrest, with its views down the long canal separating it from the house and the modern café and tea garden. Other favoured spots for the taking of tea at Wrest Park included the even more distant Hill House and the Bowling Green House.

The value of tea imported into Britain rose exponentially in the eighteenth century from £14,000 a year in 1700 to £1,777,000 by 1790, but until 1784 high taxation restricted consumption to the wealthy, with the working classes still fuelled by cheap gin. With the drastic reduction of taxation rates on tea (from 119 per cent to 12.5 per cent) in 1784 tea finally became the chosen drink of the nation. A 1797 study of the lives of the poor by Sir Frederick Eden recorded that in the cottages of Middlesex and Surrey tea was the usual beverage in the morning, the evening and at dinner, while the Duc de La Rochefoucauld recorded that, 'Throughout the whole of England the drinking of tea is general ... Though the expense is considerable, the humblest peasant has his tea twice a day like the rich man.'

The sale of loose-leafed tea enabled wealthy families to enjoy tea at home in the early eighteenth century. (Unknown artist, *c.* 1745, Yale Center for British Art)

Tea parties indoors and outdoors became the fashion for aristocratic women. (*Ladies at Tea* by Thomas Rowlandson, *c.* 1790, Yale Center for British Art)

Did you know?

Writing in John Claudius Loudon's book *The Encyclopaedia of Cottage Gardening, Husbandry and Architecture* (1834), a Mr Elles, previously gardener at Longleat House, claimed that tea was driving the cottager into poverty. Elles estimated that the expense of the tealeaves, the 'parade' of china, and the additions of milk and sugar resulted in costs of up to 2s 6d a week per household, not including, he noted, 'anything for fuel, loss of time in boiling the kettle, and in gossiping, or for breakage'.

Through the nineteenth century tea and beer were often claimed as the dual props of the labouring classes of England, whether representing work and play, the home and the alehouse, or the division between female and male enjoyments, but among the temperance and protestant non-conformists tea triumphed over the temptations of the alehouse.

By 1855 the Band of Hope was organising meetings, marches and rallies throughout the UK to encourage people to sign the pledge to abstain from all intoxicating liquors, leaving the way free for tea and coffee. From 1864 the Salvation Army also promoted abstinence on the part of its members. An association between the Liberal Party and non-conformism with its temperance sympathies in the early twentieth century brought together tea and politics rather differently from the seediness of the seventeenth-century coffee houses. With the outbreak of the First World War in 1914, restrictions on the opening hours of public houses and a rise in taxation on alcohol led to an even greater reliance on tea. Turning to a 'cuppa' in the face of disaster was said by Winston Churchill to have helped bring Britain through the Second World War, being as valuable in the fight against Hitler as ammunition. Although tea was rationed during the Second World War, those involved in essential and physical work were allocated more, as were those over the age of 70, bolstering the belief in the invigorating powers and health benefits of the drink. Through the nineteenth and twentieth centuries, through war and with peace, across religious and class divides, the pot of tea on the table and the kettle on the hob thus became a vision of England: but how did the tea garden become a part of this vision?

Stripy tents and woven basket chairs were popular features in private gardens as well as tea gardens in the nineteenth century.

These children playing at teatime reflect the central role that tea plays in British Society. (Print by Rovert Barnes, c. 1840, Yale Center for British Art)

2

Crystal Water and Copper Kettles: Eighteenth-Century Tea and Spa Gardens

By the time tea arrived in Britain in the mid-seventeenth century, London already had an array of pleasure gardens where the fashionable went to see and to be seen taking the air and indulging in a variety of refreshments. The best known of these were the Spring Gardens, Ranelegh Gardens or the famous Vauxhall. Originating as centres for *al fresco* entertainment, courting and gentle pleasures, they offered their customers bowling greens, flowered walks and concerts, and they encouraged easy social mixing. At the Spring Gardens in London, Samuel Pepys describes watching his wife's maids gathering pinks as they walked, while others recorded the warbling of birds and singing of the nightingales heard from the adjoining St James' Park. In 1654 the diarist John Evelyn noted that Mulberry Garden was 'ye only place of refreshment about ye town for persons of ye best quality to be excessively cheated at'. At all of these gardens tea was amongst the often numerous refreshments available, and by 1732 an evening spent dancing or watching fireworks in Vauxhall or Ranelagh Gardens could be finished with a refreshing cup of tea. By the mid-eighteenth century the large pleasure gardens of London had been added to by a range of

This 1790 image depicts a typical family scene at a tea garden outing, with tea things on the table and a pond and small pavilion in the background. (Print by Francis David Soiron, c. 1790, Yale Center for British Art)

9

smaller spa or spring gardens, taking their names from the chalybeate springs they formed around. These were usually smaller affairs with more limited entertainments, supposedly focusing on the health-giving properties of the waters available to drink. Some combined the often foul-tasting mineral waters with cider or ale but many preferred the innocent joys of tea drinking and even advertised themselves as such. As tea was promoted as the ideal drink for those suffering from lack of concentration, headaches, memory loss, faintness and even kidney and bladder stones, it happily sat within the concept of the health-giving spring garden and was embraced by those who found themselves feeling the ill-effects of urban living and rich foods. As early as 1667 Samuel Pepys recorded that his wife was making tea 'which Mr Pelling the potticary [apothecary] tells her is good for her cold and defluxions', and Typhoo teas were advertised as excellent for indigestion well into the twentieth century.

Did you know?

John Abercrombie, the author of one of the most influential eighteenth-century gardening books, *Every Man His Own Gardener* (1767), owned and ran The Artichoke Tea Gardens in Mile End from 1772. A few years later he took on another tea garden at Hoxton where he raised exotics and fruit. Abercrombie also designed several aristocratic gardens, wrote numerous garden books, ran a nursery and market garden in north London, and was invited to become Superintendent of the gardens of Catherine the Great. Abercrombie boasted of sixteen daughters and two sons and lived to the age of eighty: an excellent example of the cup that invigorates!

Opened in 1759, Bagnigge Wells was a typical north London spa and tea garden. It boasted two springs, one a 'chalybeate with a ferruginous character, with an agreeable subacid tartness, apt to produce a kind of giddiness and afterwards a propensity to sleep if exercise be not interposed', and the other 'a cathartic which left a distinguishable brackish bitterness on the palate', three half-pints being sufficient for most people. Perhaps because of the unpleasant taste of its spring waters, or the high price of 3*d* a cup (or 8*d* a gallon), tea drinking soon became an established part of the entertainments at Bagnigge. In the song 'A Prentice to his Mistress' the waters feature purely as decorative features while it is tea that is being consumed:

> Come prithee make it up Miss, and be as lovers be,
> We'll go to Bagnigge Wells, Miss, and there we'll have some tea;
> It's there you'll see the lady-birds perch'd on the stinging nettles,
> And chrystal water fountains and shining copper kettles;
> It's there you'll see the fishes, more curious they than whales,
> They're made of gold and silver, Miss, and wags their little tails.

The gardens at Bagnigge were more elaborate than many, perhaps owing to the proprietor's (Mr Hughes) original hobby as an amateur gardener. It is described from original sources by the author William Boulton in *The Amusements of Old London* (1901):

> The old gardens were laid out with clipped hedges of yew; formal walks ran between alleys of box and holly; there were arbours covered with sweetbrier and honeysuckle

for tea-drinking; ponds containing gold fish, then not often seen; a fountain with Cupid bestriding a swan, and leaden statues of Phyllis and Corydon.

Boulton noted that the 'severity' of the formal garden declined upon the eastern bank of the Fleet, and melted away into the pleasant rusticity of willows, elder bushes, burdock and water plants, which were well known to artists seeking opportunity for the study of natural foliage. This ideal of a rustic setting for tea-taking was one that was echoed by many contemporary tea gardens. In David Garrick's *Bon Ton, or High Life Upstairs* (1775) a city madam gives her definition of the life of fashion as 'drinking tea on summer afternoons, at Bagnigge Wells with china and gilt spoons'.

Other early tea and spa or spring gardens clustered around the Kings Cross/St Pancras area where a series of springs had long been recognised. This was also conveniently the edge of the town in the eighteenth and early nineteenth centuries – before the coming of the railway – so that the gardens constituted a trip to the countryside. A detailed description of a visit to St Chad's Wells gardens was printed in *Punch* in 1843, at which time an entrance path led from the gate to the pump room flanked by an ornamental shrubbery 'whose trees grow in the wildest luxuriance', while from the opposite end of the same room a further door led to a 'romantic wilderness'. St Chad's Wells gardens served a dual clientele, with medicinal waters in the mornings and tea in the afternoons. Tea at White Conduit gardens (near Penton Street) was served in the gardens, which included 'pleasing walks prettily disposed, genteel boxes, alcoves, clipped hedges, and avenues of shady trees', and the proprietor boasted that the milk that went into their tea and coffee came from 'cows that eat no grains', referring to the proximity of the country. Adam and Eve Tea Garden also kept cows on the adjoining meadows. Shady walks and clipped hedges along with fruit and flower gardens were the hallmarks of the Florida Gardens on the south side of Gloucester Road in south-west London and also the Flora Tea Gardens. The proprietor, Mr Hiem, grew cherries, strawberries and flowers and supplied fresh fruit, ice creams, coffee and cider, as well as the all-important teas. Cuper's Garden (near Waterloo Bridge in London), was turned into a tea garden in the mid-eighteenth century. Run by the 'Widow Evans', it was advertised as providing 'sweet enchanting sounds of the rural warblers' on a site that had provided fireworks and promenades in its more scurrilous days before health-giving tea predominated.

Did you know?

Mad for Tea?
Tea gardens are often relatively short-lived, with premises changing use to a café, inn or back to being a private residence. In Shrewsbury, the eighteenth-century tea gardens at The Hermitage and Kingsland Coffee House & Tea Gardens both went on to become asylums. The remaining Shrewsbury tea garden (Underdales) became the Pineapple Inn in 1840, offering dancing of quadrilles and seasonal strawberries.

Combined taverns and tea gardens sprung up in the nineteenth century, perhaps to cater for husband and wife outings, and had a slightly less idyllic reputation than the spa tea garden. In his 1834 *Encyclopaedia of Cottage, Farm and Villa Architecture and Furniture*, John Claudius Loudon included a design by William Ross of Bristol for a small country inn with a tea

The Monster Tea Gardens provided a typically rural feel behind its more suburban façade. (Yale Center for British Art)

garden. This was, he said, of a 'humble size', typical of the tavern tea gardens of the period, but Loudon, who was a bit of a puritan, had every hope the small tea garden would eventually expand over the skittles alley and beer gardens in the adjoining space. Ross' tea garden design included a series of alcoves with trellis-work ideally to be bedecked with honeysuckle or virgin's-bower, or where the shade or smoke of the town was too bad for these plants, ivy or Virginia creeper. A central fountain of stone or iron enlivened the tea garden, with planting of deciduous and evergreen shrubs where the 'nurseryman who supplies them does not plant more than two of a sort and that the sorts have showy or odoriferous flowers'. An excellent example of this combined tea garden and inn, which would have pleased Loudon, was Ye Olde Two Brewers at the bottom of Gold Hill in Shaftesbury. An eighteenth-century inn, the gardens had sweeping views across the Dorset countryside and catered for travellers and day trippers as well as locals. A series of photographic postcards depicts rustic chairs, rose pergolas and families enjoying tea, including perhaps the then owner who appears in several images with his dogs. The presence of a croquet set is an unusual addition, perhaps dating the images to the peak fashion for the game in the 1890s. Ye Olde Two Brewers still exists, serving pub lunches in their gardens with the same sweeping views and offering a skittle alley for those who have neglected to bring a croquet set.

At the Rosemary Tavern and Tea Gardens (London), even more frivolous activities including pony racing and tightrope walks took its clients minds off the simple pleasures of tea, and the archery ground at Princess Royal Tea Gardens harked back to its proprietor's days running the Archery Tavern. The Princess Royal Tea Gardens', advertised claim to fame was that its grounds were 'the nearest way to Kensal Green Cemetery'. In 1840 the Black Lion Tavern and Tea Garden and the Eagle Tavern with Tea Garden, along

Above: The Old Two Brewers in Shaftesbury was a combined tea garden and tavern that appears to have put an unusual emphasis on the floral delights of the tea area. (With thanks to the Devon Garden Trust)
Below: The signage for the Black Lion tavern advertised the tea gardens that can be glimpsed over the fence. (Yale Center for British Art)

Above: This Edwardian postcard hints at the daring delights of the tea garden in an age when revealing your ankle was considered scandalous.
Below: Thomas Rowlandson's 1795 image for Goldsmith's *The Vicar of Wakefield* depicts a family afternoon tea party al fresco. (Yale Center for British Art)

with over forty other taverns and tea gardens in the City of London, were refused licences by the London City Mission as being 'resorts of ill repute'. In 1860 a further attack was made on 'the east end tea gardens' in the periodical *The Builder*, which claimed they were not only of questionable artistic taste but also unsanitary and dangerous. This reputation by association tarnished the urban tea garden, which was reborn as a more innocent diversion in the countryside: the small rural tea garden replete with cottage and cottager, a sprinkling of chairs and tables on a patchwork of lawn, and refreshments to be had in the summer seasons for those with a taste for the outdoor life.

Did you know?

In Charles Dickens' *The Pickwick Papers*, Mr Pickwick's landlady pays a visit to the Spaniards Tea Gardens. The party of seven order seven cups of tea with bread and butter 'on the same scale', as Mrs Rogers declares that she could almost wish to live in the country always!

3
The Rural Retreat

From the middle of the nineteenth century a new passion for the outdoor life resulted in a demand for rural tea gardens that could cater for thirsty groups of walkers and cyclists well outside of towns and cities. Walking clubs existed formally by the 1850s and emphasised the health-enhancing effects of exercise, especially for the labouring and middle classes. Especially popular in the vicinity of manufacturing towns, the movement grew in the late Victorian and Edwardian period and the National Ramblers' Association was formed in the 1930s. Setting out for a day of innocent pleasures in the clean air, tea rather than beer was the drink of choice for the walkers, many of whom were also members of the temperance movements. The presence of women in the rambling groups also led to an emphasis on refreshments taken at tea houses and gardens or combined tavern and tea stops, as respectable women were not expected to frequent alehouses. Walkers were soon to be joined by cyclists, first tottering along on the 'high-wheelers' of the 1870s and then on the newly invented 'safety bicycle' replete with rubber tyres, chains and even gearing.

The Bicycle Touring Club (later the Cyclists' Touring Club or CTC) was founded in 1878 with an initial membership of just eighty cyclists. By 1883 membership had risen to 10,627, including the first women, and a uniform of dark green had been established. The 1890s saw the cycling craze extending to ladies' cycling clubs founded in places where the men's clubs would not accommodate them. Cycling, especially in the heavy woollen clothes worn by Victorian and Edwardian cyclists, is thirsty work and many images of early tea gardens include a bicycle or two propped against a tree or a

'Getting away from it all' is an important aspect of a tea garden visit. Here is the wonderful Beanstalk Tea Garden at Firle, near Lewes. (Image courtesy of Beanstalk Tea Garden)

Above: Walkers today still flock to tea gardens just as they did in the late nineteenth century. (Image courtesy of Falling Foss Tea Garden, Midge Hall, Whitby)

Below: By the end of the nineteenth century cycle clubs had formed all over the country, using tea gardens as their destinations. (Reproduced courtesy of Essex Record Office)

Tea Gardens, Godshill, I. W.

Two bicycles can be seen propped against the tree in this Isle of Wight tea garden.

nearby table. From 1887 onwards the CTC gave its seal of approval in the form of a cast-iron plaque (later replaced by án enamel plate showing a winged-wheel symbol) for mounting on an outside wall of hotels and restaurants that offered good accommodation and service to cyclists. The aptly named Cyclists' Rest Tea Gardens near Shoreham proudly displayed their plaque in the early 1900s. Some public houses refused to serve women wearing cycling attire and one of the Lady Cyclists' Association first initiatives was to produce a registry of approved inns and cyclists' rests suitable for women on cycling rides or tours. With the increased popularity and cheaper availability of the bicycle in the 1890s, the majority of the population could finally travel beyond the distance reached by half a day's walking. Couples and groups would set off on a weekend to explore the countryside, appreciate nature and often experience the delights of flirtation on a saddle. As a writer to the *Manchester Guardian* declared in 1895: 'We have had many pleasures in the way of travelling, but we have never yet experienced such exhilarating enthusiasm or such complete recreation. What once was impossible has become possible, and distance is no longer the barrier to the refreshment of country life or contact with kindred spirits.' Or indeed a welcome cup of tea!

For the less athletically minded, trams, trains and charabancs could also bring town-dwellers to the country. Charabancs, originally horse drawn but by 1890 usually motorised, were the favoured mode of transport for work or social group outings in the early twentieth century, making a comeback in the Second World War. Open-topped and seating as many as twenty people, they could ensure the survival of a favoured tea garden with repeat excursions run by the charabanc company. Trams and buses also reached to the edges of towns and beyond: in 1908 the sender of a postcard illustrating the 'Shady Corner at the Rustic Tea Gardens' in Saltash, recorded, 'Came out by tram to Saltash and home by steamer, Just had a lovely tea'.

The tea gardens at Ash Platt (also known as Robert's Tea Garden) advertised in about 1915 that they could be reached by 'Quarter-hours walk from Green St. Green; Half Hour's walk from Bus terminus, Farnborough'. They also noted that the gardens were laid out in 'The Old Stile [*sic*]', suggesting there was already a recognised 'tea garden style' for these rural refreshment stops. It was not until the 1930s that private cars became a common means for days out in the countryside for the wealthy, and so shared outings were the norm through the late nineteenth and early twentieth centuries.

Did you know?

Messages from the Garden

Postcards are invaluable for finding out about tea gardens, but the messages on them can also provide insights into their visitors and their enjoyments. The writer of a card from the tea garden at The Green Man in Edgware appears to have been a connoisseur of tea gardens: '*We went to Eastcote [tea garden] yesterday & had a grand time. Cannot get cards from there as it is such a small place. This is a corner of the tea gardens at our suburban quarters, so you can just imagine we have a fine time here at our garden parties. Uncle John.*' The Eastcote Tea Gardens were in Pinner, Middlesex, and were combined with the local post office, so it is surprising there were no cards to post.

Larger parties of day trippers would commandeer charabancs, such as this group at Hankham Tea Gardens.

Jenner's Tea Garden in Bramber specialised in providing refreshments for larger parties visiting the picturesque West Sussex village.

As tea gardens became increasingly popular, disused laborers' cottages, keepers' lodges or even old stables were converted to tea houses as they fell vacant. The tea gardens at Carnewas (near Truro) started life as a mining stable in its cliffside setting, with the adjoining gardens as a paddock for the ponies, while Falling Foss Tea Gardens were started on the lawns of the gamekeeper's cottage by his wife. Following in long tradition, it was the view of the nearby Bedruthan steps, now owned by the National Trust, which inspired the adaptation to serve teas at Carnewas. Occupants of larger houses or farms turned out their tables onto the lawns en masse to make the most of visitors as nostalgia for the countryside became a fashion of the early twentieth century. Basing its attractions on nearby sites and scenery and convenient halting places for the rural 'tourist', the location of a tea garden was vital to its success. Particularly attractive villages or known beauty spots often had clusters of tea gardens catering for visitors pouring out of the towns at weekends. Bramber (West Sussex) may hold the record for the number of tea gardens in one small village. Replete with a castle and a railway station and within easy reach for day trips from Worthing by charabanc or cycle, the village was a mecca for outings. Bramber Station even had an especially long platform to cope with the numbers of arrivals. In response to the demand as many as seven tea gardens were active in the fifteen years before the First World War. They included J. Keywood's Tea Gardens, Hollis's Temperance Hotel and Tea Gardens, Old Cottage Tea Gardens (with covered bowers and shelters), Yew Tree/Jenner's Tea Gardens (by 1912), and Alfred Friar's Tea Gardens by 1901. Keywood's was run by James Keywood, who was also a carpenter, and his wife (a laundress), and boasted 'Large and Small Parties Catered

For/Accommodation for Cyclists', while the Old Cottage Tea Gardens also welcomed 'Sunday Schools, Band of Hope, Choirs, Cyclists etc.', perhaps competing with the Hollis Temperance Tea Gardens. Lee in North Devon, a picturesque village sandwiched between the rugged coast of the Lee Bay and the delights of the 'Fuschia Valley', also boasted several tea gardens that lasted until the 1980s. Also in Devon, Maidencombe sprouted several tea gardens (including Bungalow Tea Gardens, Ferndale Tea Gardens, and Maidencombe Farm Tea Gardens) to cater for the tourists who could enjoy both the countryside and the beaches. The Radford Grove Tea Gardens close to Radford Folly, Nottingham, was a favourite destination for the town's inhabitants as early as the 1830s and was notable for the fine view of Wollaton Hall, although visitors also had the choice of the Carrington Tea Gardens (until its sale in 1864) or the Lenton Grove combined tavern, tea gardens and baths.

Did you know?

Bankruptcy by Tea

Keeping a tea garden was not always a successful trade, despite attracting people from other trades. Thomas Blackburn, who had been a tallow-chandler in Liverpool, changed careers to become a tea garden-keeper in Seacombe, Chester. However, it appears he may not have been a success in either trade as he was named a bankrupt in *The Law Advertiser* on 26 August 1824.

Riverside gardens were always popular and local boat hire meant that the tea gardens had a 'captive' clientele with people queueing for boats at busy times or waiting for friends to return from boat trips. They also provided an excellent spot to pass commentary on other river users. The long-lived Marlow Bridge Tea Gardens satisfied all these, along with a view of the famous church on the other side of the river. Tea gardens at Arundel, (Sussex), Fordingbridge (Hampshire), Newlyn and Ball Tea Gardens in Tuckton (Christchurch, Dorset) and the Ruswarp Chain Bridge Riverside Gardens all offered boat hire as well as tea. At the Orchard Tea Gardens in Grantchester students and dons arrived by bicycle or punted along the River Cam, as they still do today, combining the delights of

The Falling Foss Tea Garden is named after the dramatic waterfall close by that has attracted visitors since the nineteenth century. The tea garden is now staffed by 'Team Foss'! (Courtesy of Falling Foss Tea Garden, Midge Hall, Whitby)

the scenic journey with the joy of the destination. Vinson's Tea Lawns in Sussex also owed their success to their riverside location and the view of the famous stone bridge over the River Arun. Beese's Tea Gardens in Bristol was founded in 1846 by Mrs Beese, who saw the opportunity to provide refreshments to the many travellers using the Conham Ferry, the captain of which was coincidentally Mr Beese. Flatford Cottage Tea Gardens (Suffolk) were fortunate in combing three of the most important factors for success: a rustic cottage, a riverside location, and the known tourist attraction of Flatford Mill, associated with the painter John Constable. The Oast House and Tea Terrace at Horeham Road, East Sussex, allowed visitors to sit within the picturesque walls of the oast house complex. At Hadleigh in Essex the Castle Retreat Tea Gardens perhaps catered for those who could stand no more of Hadleigh's romantic ruined castle.

Tea gardens in popular locations could become overwhelmed with visitors and some expanded well beyond their original scale with accommodation, garaging, and a wider range of refreshments and food. Little Ashe Gardens boasted that they had been visited by 20,000 persons in one summer, while a message on a postcard from Litlington Tea Gardens in about 1900 boasted, 'Lovely picnic to-day, drove in three large char-a-bancs, nearly a hundred of us'. The Mead Tea Gardens (Bath) catered for an estimated 84,000 customers between its opening in 1923 and the eve of the Second World War. A further 100,000 visited between 1939 and 1950, reflecting the proximity of the town of Bath and the ability of customers to get out to the gardens despite petrol rationing. The attractions included the valley and brook, St Catherine's Court and church, as well as an existing market garden in 1923. Unusually lasting through the two wars and into the 1990s (with later openings for charity), The Mead was described by the *Bath Chronicle* at its opening in June 1923: 'It is not only that the house is a picturesque old place, that its extensive gardens are aglow with sweet-scented flowers, that the scenery all around is of wondrous beauty, but, over and above all this, the actual teas provided are a sheer delight'.

Above: Flatford Mill Tea Garden drew visitors from the river and the surrounding countryside to enjoy the famous scene.
Below: This image of one of the many Litlington tea gardens captures a tranquil inter-war atmosphere.

LITLINGTON TEA GARDENS, SUSSEX.   D 14610

Above: Hyde Park Tea Gardens drew a different class of clientele than most of the small-scale rural tea gardens.
Below: The tea house and gardens at Harrogate Valley were packed with visitors on summer weekends and it is difficult to see how anyone could have been served. Steamer chairs as well as deckchairs were available.

Typical rural tea gardens were often very small, occupying only the front lawn of the cottager who had decided to cash in on the craze for country outings. Those that catered for charabanc parties were the exceptions, although their names have come to dominate the history of the tea garden. However, urban or suburban tea gardens that could rely on a constant clientele through the season also expanded through the Edwardian era and inter-war years often as an adjunct to the public park with its refreshment pavilion and bandstands. Offering music and sometimes dancing, these gardens were typified by matching chairs and tables, professional waiters and waitresses, a wider menu and longer opening hours than the rural front garden. Hyde Park in central London had a tea garden underneath the shelter of mature trees, and Kew Gardens' refreshment pavilion spilled out over the lawns, giving tea drinkers the unusual sight of the Chinese Pagoda in the distance. At the famous Valley Gardens in Harrogate the creation of pleasure gardens, scenic walks, a boating lake and a bandstand created demand for a suitably thatched wooden tea house and tea gardens to complement the original Pump Rooms. Hundreds of people enjoyed teas in the colourful steamer chairs and deckchairs, with a band and dancing included as part of the day's festivities. Retreating indoors for the colder seasons, the 'winter gardens' of hotels also hosted afternoon tea dances, and in turn took on the slightly rustic appearance of the genuine tea garden. The tea dance gave rise to the distinctive 'tea dress' suitable for afternoon wear but allowing movement for dancing, a fashion which thrived through the 1930s and '40s and had a revival in the nostalgic early twenty-first century.

As the private car came to dominate over the bicycle (or charabanc) in the 1930s and 1950s, so the location of tea gardens shifted. The car allowed a greater degree of freedom, which meant that tea might be taken in isolated spots previously unlikely to attract much passing trade. Large parking areas, rarely available in small villages, also became an important consideration. Extended laybys at the summit of twisting hill roads were a favourite location for pull-in café/tea gardens with extensive views and a calming cup of tea for the nervous driver (or passenger) before the descent either onwards or back down. Isolated inns previously serving horse-drawn coaches who had been caught in bad weather sprouted purpose-made matching sets of chairs and parasols. These mid- to late twentieth-century tea gardens were often more perfunctory in their 'garden' aspect, emphasising instead the opportunity to stretch the legs, relax from the stress of driving and of course visit the lavatories, and there was little of the rustic in their appearance.

4
What's in a Name?

The naming of a tea garden could be key to its success and also gives us a clue to the styles that were favoured at different periods. In the early to mid-nineteenth century, when many tea gardens were combined with taverns, the gardens would merely become an 'adjunct' to the name of the tavern or inn: the Bagnigge Wells Tavern and Tea Gardens for example, or the York and Albany Tavern and Tea Gardens (both in London). However, by the Edwardian period most tea gardens relied on customers pouring out of towns on day trips to enjoy the countryside and so names increasingly had a rural theme. Keeping the 'cottage' element was a favourite ploy, with examples including Honeysuckle Tea Cottage and Gardens (Hampshire), Apple Tree Cottage Tea Gardens (Cornwall), Ivy Cottage Tea Gardens (Bispham, Lancashire), The Contentment Cottage (Buxton, Derby). The Sparrow's Nest Tea Gardens in Lowestoft may have been named either from an original cottage or from their very small size. Being of small size appears to have been one of the attractions of the rural tea garden, giving it a sort of 'secret' feel, which also appealed to young couples, such as the Cosy Corner Tea Gardens in Cleethorpes, run between the wars by a Mrs Wilkinson, or Pretty Corner Tea Gardens (Norfolk), which are still running today. The two 'Hermitage' Tea Gardens (one in Shrewsbury and one in Knaresborough) might be taking the ideal of the tea garden as rural retreat a little too far. A name that hinted at previous, preferably rustic usages of the building attached to the gardens could also conjure up the countryside for weary urban dwellers: The Old Forge Tea Gardens in Birdlip (Gloucestershire), the Old Mill House Tea Garden (Wannock, East Sussex), the Millcroft Fruit Garden Tea Rooms (Norden, Lancashire), the Oast House Tea Terrace (East Sussex) and the Old Rectory Tea Gardens (St Colomb Major) – the latter presuming the vicar was not branching out into teas himself. The blatantly titled Rustic Tea Gardens in Saltash (Cornwall) were possibly the same as the Saltash Apple Tree Tea Gardens, which featured a gothic-style cottage as well as old apple trees in the front garden area. Flower and tree names were especially attractive, hinting at both the countryside and the garden elements of the tea

Did you know?

The Story of the Cingalee
Most tea gardens are named after a nearby tourist attraction, a traditional English flower or a generally 'cottagey' name; however, the Cingalee Restaurant and Tea Garden in Hadleigh, Essex, was probably named after the 1904 musical *Cingalee*. Staged in the West End, the story took place on a colonial tea plantation in Ceylon (now Sri Lanka) and one of the most successful songs from the musical was entitled 'Tea, tea, tea'. In 1912 the Southend Operatic & Dramatic Society were the first ever amateur group to perform the musical and one can only presume that one of the actors/singers or a member of the audience was then responsible for the naming of the Cingalee Restaurant and Tea Garden.

Above: Pretty Corner Tea Rooms and Gardens were first established in 1926 to cater for visitors to this popular part of the Norfolk coast. (Courtesy of Pretty Garden Café and Tea Gardens)
Below: Today Pretty Corner continues to attract visitors and still reflects the original ideal of the tea garden. (Courtesy of Pretty Garden Café and Tea Gardens)

garden and tea garden names include apple, cedar, honeysuckle, ivy, myrtle, rose, shamrock, yew, and the rather wonderful Lettuce Leaf Tea Gardens at Dunnose Cottage, Shanklin (Isle of Wight), as well as the modern Beanstalk Tea Garden near Lewes, East Sussex.

Pointing out a connection between the location of the tea garden and a well-known tourist attraction also helped to entice people, as at the Flatford Mill Tea Garden (Suffolk), the Chain Bridge Tea Gardens in Ruswarp (North Yorkshire), Lee Abbey Tea Gardens (Devon), the Sonning Lock Tea Garden (Berkshire) or the Fuchsia Glen Tea Gardens (Ilfracombe, North Devon). The Banks O' Doon Tea Gardens (Scotland) traded on its connection with Robert Burns via his verses on the bridge, as well as the views of the 'Brig' itself. The Lorna Doone Farm and Tea Garden did the same for the fictional character on Exmoor, while the Robin Hood Tea Gardens were rather oddly situated in Epping (Essex) and boasted a fine set of lupins. The Landslip Tea Gardens on the Isle of Wight appeared to be making a selling point out of the unstable cliffs at Ventnor, while the large Abbey View Tea Gardens in Tewkesbury (Gloucestershire) were so close to the abbey itself that the rather odd collection of statues that dotted the gardens might have been mistaken for ghostly ecclesiastical visitors in search of refreshment, although the central exotic pavilion topped by a classical figure gave pause for thought.

Sometimes there appears to be a mismatch between the name and the appearance of the gardens themselves. The Enchanted Cottage Tea Garden in Lyndhurst, for example, was based in what appears to be a rather solidly un-enchanting brick-built 'villa', albeit in the desirable destination of the New Forest. By the mid-twentieth century, when many tea gardens were relocating away from small villages to locations with better opportunities for parking, names appear to get ever more removed from reality. The Monk's Rest Tea Gardens in Worlebury (Somerset) was a modern café with extensive car parking and views of the caravan sites in the valley below, while the Olde Worlde Tea Gardens on the Isle of Wight were neither old nor 'olde', and by the 1970s the Cosy Nook Tea Garden in Crantock (Cornwall) was mostly comprised of crazy paving and only cosy in scale, although it now combines some of the

Robin Hood Gardens, Epping.

Robin Hood is traditionally associated with Sherwood Forest so the naming of this tea garden on the edge of Epping Forest is somewhat of a mystery. It is now a country pub with beer rather than tea served in the gardens.

best cakes in Cornwall with being an art gallery and tea gardens! The Bungalow Tea Gardens at Maidencombe (Devon) had a rustic appearance that would not now be generally associated with the term 'bungalow', although as these gardens firmly predate the spread of the 1950s suburban bungalow they may be recalling the Indian colonial origins of tea and bungalows. If all else failed the tea gardens became known by the name of the proprietor, although this causes confusion for any local or tea garden historian. Of the seven known names of tea gardens in Bramber (West Sussex) between 1900 and 1915, three took the names of their proprietors: Jenner's, Keywood's, and Alfred Friar's. Similarly, using the name of the village as a sole title could

Statues are rarely seen in tea gardens and so the proliferation at the Abbey Tea Gardens in Tewkesbury must have been inspired by the nearby Abbey. These tea gardens were very upmarket with matching chairs and tables and finely decorated shelters running along the sides.

cause confusion in popular villages with the possibility of several gardens going by the same name, such as at the several Salcombe Regis Tea Gardens (Devon) or Hankham Tea Gardens (East Sussex). In Godshill (Isle of Wight), the Cottage Tea Gardens are probably the same as the Leal's Tea Gardens, and may even have turned eventually into the Olde World Tea Gardens.

Occasional oddities do exist to intrigue the historian, one such being the Ace of Diamonds Tea Gardens in Bodfari, Denbighshire. Nothing in the 1930s' images of the peaceful well-kept lawn with its canvas and wooden chairs, parasols and tea things spread on tablecloths gives a hint of gambling and the card shark. Similarly confusing are the Symonds Yat Alpine Cottage and Tea Gardens: distinctively un-Alpine architecturally, they perhaps played on their location in the picturesque Wye Valley, which had been ambitiously compared in the eighteenth century to the Swiss landscape. Also geographically confused was the Shamrock Tea House and Gardens, located on the Isle of Wight rather than in Ireland as one might have expected.

In the 1970s and '80s Cosy Nook displayed typical bright colours and Coca-Cola parasols along with its then fashionable crazy paving.

Attracting customers to a tea garden depended on both location and advertising. For those that sprung up in locations already known for their tourist attractions, a small sign or a name painted on the house itself was sufficient to attract trade, while those on the highway or facing onto a river might even rely purely on the presence of tables and chairs to announce their presence. A large and popular tea garden, such as the one at the Steven's Landing Stage (Abingdon), might invest money in more stylish signage; a postcard of 1908 shows archways proclaiming the name of the gardens facing onto the river and also toward the landing stage. Dual-purpose hostelries or combined shops and tea gardens made use of their sizeable frontages and already commercial nature to affix larger signs. The Bell Inn in Minster (Kent) gave as much prominence to its tea garden advertisement as it did to its more traditional role as an inn, although the latter might be taken for granted in its name. The same was true of the Old Royal Oak public house (Paddington), which had a large sign across the wall or fence leading to the rear gardens. Woodlands Tea Garden (Sussex) with its large house and garden benefitted from a large advertisement painted on some kind of canvas and attached across the front railings, which hints at the seasonal nature of the tea garden there. Minimal outlay appears to have been the usual rule for the smaller tea gardens, with a sign painted on the side of the house nearest to the entrance, possibly supplemented by a homemade board

Ivy Cottage, Bispham. 21/6/0

Above: Many smaller tea gardens painted their signs on the sides of buildings or even the roof, as here at Ivy Cottage, Bispham.
Below: The chimney stack at Lee Abbey tea garden left little room for anything other than the word 'TEAS'.

THE COTTAGE AND TEA GARDEN, LEE ABBEY

This wonderful image has a mystery attached as nothing else is known of Mr West's Tea Garden other than it boasted a topiary teapot and was open for business in 1909. (Courtesy of the Garden Museum, London)

by the gate. The Brightstone Tea Gardens (Isle of Wight) had their name emblazoned across the end of the tea pavilion in an unusually bold style in keeping with the sparse look of the site, but also possibly as a response to the number of competing tea gardens on the island. White lettering in bold capitals was favoured by the Waltham Tea Gardens which, by the number of people shown outside on its advertising card, appear to have been large enough to cater for charabancs and cycling parties. Ivy Cottage Tea Gardens in Bispham (Lancashire) benefitted from passing road trade and, as well as featuring a sign painted on the side of the house, an advertising board was placed prominently on the verge by the entrance. Chimneys were also useful for painted signs, as at the Lee Abbey Tea Gardens (Devon), where the sign on the stone stack announced simply 'Tea'. Arun Tea Gardens (Sussex) appears to have painted its sign across the roof tiles of the 'porch'. For the very smallest garden a tea sign tacked up on a tree would suffice to entice ramblers, as at Coysh's Tea Gardens in Maidencombe or the Fairlight Glen Tea Gardens, the latter of which appear to have been little more than a table and chairs in a shady spot with a converted building as servery. At the steep and crowded village of Lynmouth in Devon the tea gardens flew a flag which made the best use of space and could also be seen by those hiking on the hills either side of the village. The flag outside the Dartmoor Dairies Tea Gardens (Devon) would have been readily seen on most days but sadly was hanging limp with no wind when photographed for a postcard image. A photograph labelled as 'Mr West's Surrey' and dated 1909 depicts several tables and chairs in a garden with a large topiary teapot, which may well be a combined advertising sign and garden decoration. Wooden signs in the instantly recognisable shape of teapots were frequently hung or placed by the roadside and are making a comeback in the twenty-first century. In the 1950s and '60s, Wall's Ice Cream appear to have 'donated' signs for its ice cream to some tea gardens to hang out as a temptation to passers-by. Ye Olde Worlde Tea Gardens in Bosherston (Wales) used this rather than a name board, and the crowded 1960s tea lawns at Houghton also had signs for Wall's.

Other than signs at the tea garden itself, postcards, presumably produced or at least sanctioned by the proprietors of the various tea gardens, appear to have been the main method of advertising. They often depict a favoured view replete with tables and chairs, although often staged with no customers. The Castle Retreat Gardens at Hadleigh is an example of this type, boasting six tables and a longer trestle under cover, the tables had been thoughtfully provided with small vases of flowers for the occasion of the photograph. Carefully ironed tablecloths and a single laid table testify to the care of the composition, with a single 'waiter' (perhaps the proprietor or his wife) shown at a discrete distance, waiting eagerly to serve the customers. In handwritten style the advertising cards emphasise the small-scale traditional nature of the tea garden and rarely provide

Although most images of Victorian and Edwardian gardens are in delightful sepia tones, some sought to attract customers with coloured images. Wannock Tea Gardens were among the largest and best known for their flowers, justifying this extra expense.

more in the way of location than the name of the garden or the nearest village. Even the smallest of tea gardens, which boasted little more than two or three tables, appear to have

Did you know?

Between its invention in 1907 and the early 1930s, colour images of tea gardens were often created by a process called autochrome. The process involved covering a glass plate with a thin wash of tiny potato starch grains dyed red, green and blue, thus creating a filter. A thin layer of emulsion was added over that. When the plate was flipped and exposed to light, the resulting image could be developed into a transparency. It seems appropriate that gardens famous for providing sustenance should be captured for eternity using potatoes.

HAVING TEA AT WANNOCK GARDENS

Above: Anyone that lived in Britain in the 1970s will instantly recognise the PG Tips chimps, although here thankfully in concrete – one of the many attractions of the Wannock Tea Gardens. Surprisingly few tea gardens included gnomes or other figures in the gardens.
Below: The message on the back of this unusual card from Badgers Holt Tea Gardens at Dartmeet (Devon) declares that it is 'right on the water's edge' and the only trouble with the gardens was that there was 'too much to eat'!

CRYSTAL TEA GARDENS, ALTON, STAFFORDSHIRE.—The public are most respectfully informed that these GROUNDS are NOW OPEN for the reception of visitors. Admission by refreshment ticket, 6d. each. Parties bringing their own rations will be provided with accommodation for luncheon at the charge of 2d. per head ; also with hot water and tea service on the same terms.

Convenient arrangements have been made for most of the popular sports, as Bowling, Skittles, Quoits, &c.

The gardens are within five minutes' walk of the Alton Railway Station on the North Staffordshire Line.

Alton, July 14, 1853.

N.B.—General SEED DEPOT.—MELONS and CUCUMBERS grown for sale.

Newspaper advertisements, usually only for larger establishments, are an underused but valuable resource for the history of tea gardens.

had cards made, reflecting the 'postcard craze' in the first decades of the twentieth century. A few tea gardens had paintings made of the gardens to use as images while others resorted to hand-colouring, enlivening the more usual sepia tones or, from about 1910, a form of colour photography known as autochrome.

Some of the more successful gardens also branched out into 'humorous' advertising cards, perhaps assured that their real-life attractions were already well known. In the 1970s Wannock Tea Gardens made a publicity postcard of chimps having tea in the gardens, referencing the successful PG Tips advertising campaign of the period, although the Wannock chimps were made of concrete rather than hired from the local zoo. Newspaper advertising was an expense that only the larger gardens could consider. In fact, the numbers of visitors to their gardens often appeared as a feature of the advertisement, alongside 'refreshing' teas, proximity to rivers or tourist attractions, and suitability for group outings, Sunday school trips or cyclists. Again Little Ash was at the forefront of this with regular advertisements boasting 'Beautiful Grounds, Meadow, Swings, Roundabouts, High Class Teas and Refreshments. Visited by 20,000 persons last Summer!' In June 1857 the tea gardens at Trentham Inn made use of the *Staffordshire Advertiser* to announce their seasonal openings and the presence of a Quadrille band, as well as the proximity to Trentham Park, while the Crystal Tea Gardens in Alton (Staffordshire) also used the *Advertiser* to tempt people to their tea service along with the offer of skittles, bowls and quoits in the summer of 1857.

5
Gardens, Fashions and Furnishings

Although by definition the tea garden was almost always set within a garden of some kind the extent of any actual planting varied considerably. Many proprietors appear to have done very little in the way of enhancing the gardens, instead favouring larger areas of lawn or grass under established orchard trees. This was obviously practical as large numbers of visitors and flowerbeds often do not mix well, while the small scale of many of the enterprises appealed to those with little money to spare and combining summertime profits with practical fruit production later in the year was an obvious choice. The spring blossom of the orchard also appealed to early visitors, as is still the case at the Orchard Tea Gardens in Grantchester. An early recognition of the possibilities offered by an orchard are recorded in an 1822 advertisement held in the Staffordshire Record Office for Perry Croft House in Tamworth. The hopeful agent recorded that 'the orchard is well stocked with choice fruit trees, which have recently come into full bearing, the garden is exceedingly

This vintage shelter at Litlington Tea Garden recalls the wooden alcoves and pavilions that were used in tea and spa gardens from the eighteenth century onwards to escape the rain and perhaps engage in a little flirtation. (Courtesy of Litlington Tea Garden)

productive as a market garden, and might with advantage be converted into Fruit, Flower and Tea Gardens.' Dale Cottage in Milton Abbas and the more famous Bosherton gardens were both perfect examples of a cottage with a small lawn that turned into a tea garden in the summer, with visitors crowded on to what little space there was and enjoying the ad hoc atmosphere. Like many, Whitpot Mill Tea Gardens (Devon) appear to have started life as a casual arrangements of tables and chairs in an orchard setting, transforming (or perhaps extending) over time to a more designed garden with gravel walks, climbing roses and wooden alcoves.

Roses growing over house walls, pergolas and arches were one of the most popular flowers in the tea garden, fitting both with the rustic and cottagey feel and matching their flowering to the short-lived season. Rambling roses can be seen in numerous tea gardens, including the famous Hankham Tea Gardens (Sussex), and Newlyn and Ball (Dorset), and unsurprisingly at the Rose Tea Gardens at Watford Heath (Hertfordshire). The Old Farm Fuchsia Glen Tea Gardens at Lee on Sea (Ilfracombe) was crowded with shrubs, and the house itself overwhelmed with climbing roses. The Robin Hood Garden in Epping boasted a fine show of lupins, while also in Essex the St Osyth Kingsland Tea Gardens were advertised as the 'Tea and Flower Gardens' and appear to have lived up to their name. Frenchays garden at Cleeve distinguished itself from the several other tea gardens in the village by its large conservatory and immaculate beds of flowers, seen in numerous images being maintained by a gardener-cum-waiter. The annual bedding style was also favoured at the Old Rectory Tea Gardens at Orme. Wellesbourne Tea Gardens near Warwick had an enthusiastic horticultural hand at the helm as by the 1930s it included pergolas, rockeries, a lily pond, crazy paving terraces, shrubs and (almost as an afterthought) a small flat lawn area set aside for teas.

Starting life as a small tea garden in an orchard setting, the Kingsland Tea Gardens in St Osyth obviously invested much time and effort in creating a flower-filled setting, becoming the Tea and Flower Gardens.

Part of Tea Gardens, St. Osyth.

Images of children playing in tea gardens are rare, making this view of St Osyth's extensive flower gardens especially important.

Another garden that placed a higher than usual emphasis on the floral aspect was the Litlington Tea Garden in East Sussex (still in existence today). This boasted a monkey puzzle tree close to the entrance as well as further tree and shrub planting. Ferns, although in keeping with the rustic nature of gardens and certainly easy to maintain, do not appear to have been popular, perhaps due to their predisposition for a gloomy or damp atmosphere – the Ferry Cottage Tea Garden in the ferny Lake Windermere (Cumbria) district and the Pretty Corner in the sandy area of Sheringham (Norfolk) being exceptions to the rule.

More unusual garden designs reflect the predilections of the owner. A stone or rockwork fountain can just be glimpsed in a postcard of the Bungalow Gardens in the early twentieth century, and a rock garden and pool attracted clients at the Garwick Glen Tea Garden (Isle of Man). Rockwork was also present at The Contentment Cottage tea garden in Buxton. Wilmington Tea Garden (now the Wishing Well Tea Rooms and Garden) boasted a rare wishing well as one might expect and the *Bath Chronicle* recorded another wishing well at the Mead Tea Garden in the 1920s. The tea gardens at Menai (South Wales) had a large gnome in 1932 and a later coloured image depicts an entire tableaux by the front of the relatively modern bungalow-style building (ironically named Ye Olde Tea Gardens), at a time when gnomes were beginning their slow social descent from the Edwardian country house to the pleasure gardens and suburbs. Rather more surprisingly, the tea garden at Godshill (Isle of Wight) had a selection of what appear to be pottery terriers at the end of the path to the tea rooms.

Brandreth Bagshawe, proprietor of The Cottage of Content tea gardens on the appropriately named Fern Road, Buxton, was an example of a professional gardener turned tea garden owner, a combination which appears to have been more common in the early years of the tea garden and tavern than during the nineteenth century. At his death (aged seventy-eight) in 1844 it was said: 'His cottage was always neatly decked out, and his adjoining garden kept in excellent order; and being abundantly supplied with grottos [rockwork] etc. it was much resorted to in the season as a sort of tea garden by the visitors, to whom Brandreth was an object of interest.' The furniture within the garden was also detailed in a later history of the area as comprising 'rustic and fanciful summer-houses … tables, chairs and seats, in unison- all painted in harlequin colours. The diminutive, but elegant parterres, have a pretty effect, and altogether it presents an air of clean quiet beauty'.

Dishdolls' Tea Gardens from the Terrace, Rawcliffe, Nr. Blackpool

Above: The oddly named Dishdolls Tea Gardens boasted a central pool and also seems to have welcomed children by the 1950s.
Below: A gardener-cum-waiter can be seen tending the plants at Frenchay Tea Gardens near Bristol.

The Tea Gardens,   Frenchay, near Bristol.

Jones' Ye Olde Tea Gardens, Menai Bridge.

FRITH.
MBGE.159

A rare glimpse of a gnome at this unusual Welsh tea garden. A sign on a building further up proclaims 'Luncheons available'.

Did you know?

In 1825, a book on the attractions of Macclesfield suggested that its readers would be 'highly delighted with Mr. Hammond's Tea Gardens; these gardens though small, do great credit to the owner, in his skilful taste of miniaturing different places in foreign climes...'

In regard to furniture, a scatter of mismatched bentwood chairs, dining table chairs and school-style chairs often indicate a smaller or more short-lived concern, with an owner unsure or unwilling to commit to purpose-made outdoor furniture. At the tiny Castle Retreat Tea Gardens in Hadleigh the chairs appear to have been brought out of the proprietor's own house, while the Cooden Tea Gardens in East Sussex could barely fit any furnishings in at all. The Rustic Tea Gardens in Saltash lived up to its name as far as furnishings were concerned with a simple planking table on top of a sawn tree trunk, and benches that appear to have the bark still on them. This simple wooden furnishing and matching tree trunk pergolas reflected late Victorian fashion and also eased the monetary outlay, although the extreme rustic nature of the chairs at the Bungalow Tea Gardens at Maidencombe (Devon) might give visitors little faith in their ability to hold up. When outdoor furniture was purchased, folding wooden deck- or steamer chairs were the most popular. Some of the chairs at Wingrave Tea Gardens, at the popular Burnham Beeches, were caught 'mid-fold' in a photograph probably dating to the 1910–1920s period and showing the gardens busy with couples and also small groups of men. Steamer chairs were especially popular in the 1900–1930s period, with inbuilt sunshades sheltering women's faces from the harmful effects of the sun, in a period when pale complexions were the fashion. Drusilla's Tea Garden in Berwick (East Sussex) was unusual in having woven armchairs and tables despite its small scale and the lavender-hedged walkway there also hints at a degree of floral design above the usual. The Old Mill House in Wannock (East Sussex) had a combination of basket chairs and folding chairs within its quite substantial gardens. Large planters and purpose-made thatched shelters for rows of tables and chairs would have extended the seasons here, as well as the numbers that could be entertained, and delights included a mill pond and rustic bridge. Tents and arbours, popular with couples, were decorated with trellis and set around the edges of the garden in sequestered spots. The presence of several discrete pavilions for courting couples may also have contributed to the success of the Pavilion Tea Gardens in Derby, and when sold in 1849 the description notes: 'Five elegant PAVILIONS fitted in the rustic style, with Tables etc. complete.'

Table umbrellas are rarely seen in the smaller tea gardens of the Victorian and Edwardian period, seemingly reserved for large establishments such as the tea gardens in Kensington Gardens (which also boasted woven armchairs), but by the 1930s they had crept in to smaller gardens such as the Badger's Holt Tea Garden, (Dartmeet), Robert's Tea Gardens (Bodelwyddan) and the tea gardens at Saltburn-by-the-Sea (Cleveland). Cheaper, colourful materials from the 1960s onwards changed the look of the tea garden with stripy parasols at every table and advertisement for Coca-Cola or even Cinzano by the 1970s. A photograph that appears to have been taken especially for use as an 'advertisement card' for the Castle Retreat Tea Gardens at Hadleigh depicts each table with a neat tablecloth and a large vase

The very smallest of tea gardens hardly had room for flowers or signs.

Above: Only the small sign on the fence alerts the passer-by that this is anything more than a flower-filled cottage garden. (Courtesy of the Garden Museum)
Below: Traditional steamer chairs were an expensive investment for the smaller tea garden.

Coach & Horses Tea Gardens, Sedlescombe.

of flowers but the absence of visitors and the pose of the serving maid suggest that the image was very likely posed as a one-off. For the smaller gardens providing flower arrangements on the tables every day would have soon resulted in empty flowerbeds and it was a luxury that was not really expected in this period, except at the highest class of establishment.

Rather mysteriously, images of tea gardens rarely seem to include children or any play areas set aside for them. An emphasis on customers who arrived by hiking or cycling or in works' outing charabancs may of course have resulted in fewer children in the gardens. That they did come to the gardens is evidenced by advertisements aimed at 'Sunday Schools' – although these youngsters may have been expected to sit demurely at the tables. In Nottinghamshire the Rosary Tea Gardens (Burton Joyce) had a sturdy set of swings, and Little Ash Tea Gardens in Plymouth specifically advertised the presence of

Modern tea gardens also use a range of chairs, here favouring the traditional rustic look. (Courtesy of Beanstalk Tea Garden)

swings, roundabout and seesaw, as well as its suitability for Sunday school outings. At the tiny cottage tea gardens at Nant-Y-Coed in Llanfairfechan a postcard depicts children playing on improvised seesaws.

Also absent from images of most tea gardens are any indication of food. No triple-tiered platters of sandwiches and cakes, piles of strawberries, scones, or slices of Victoria Sandwich appear in the early images of tea garden tables, although a glimpse of knives and side plates hint at something more than liquid refreshments. In 1901 the writer William Boulton referred to the tea gardens' 'harmless dissipations of the teapot and muffin' and a depiction of an amorous couple in a tea garden alcove in the 1830s does appear to show two small buns or muffins on the table. The Mead Tea Gardens near Bath is recorded as having served a complete range of griddle cakes, scones, cream, fruit and teas as well as selling fruits 'culled from the gardens'. In Devon and Cornwall the scone would have been the natural accompaniment to tea and is recorded in oral memories of tea gardens by the mid-twentieth century. However, smaller gardens may have felt that baking was a step too far in investment of funds for what could be an irregular clientele. The Crystal Tea Gardens near Alton advertised 'facilities for eating' at 2d per person, but in 1853 expected visitors to 'bring their own rations'. Similarly the diminutive Cottage of Contentment Tea Garden in Buxton was noted as providing tea and 'a sparkling glass' of refreshment, but 'parties [must] take their own provisions'. A large cake features in an image of Ye Two Brewers (Shaftesbury) but although the inn also functioned as a tea garden the particular images suggest a private party of some kind. In 1927 a postcard from the tea garden at Badgers Holt declared that there was 'too much to eat', although sadly it does not elaborate what! The term 'tea' can of course cover both the beverage itself and the food that attends it, and so we are often left to imagine what the term 'teas and refreshments' actually covered prior to the 1950s.

Above: A rare glimpse of children's play equipment in a tea garden in Wales.
Left: Scones and cream gateaux were on the menu in Devon in the 1960s.

Above: Scones or plain muffins and tea were the standard fare for the traditional tea garden. (Courtesy of The Orchard Tea Garden, Grantchester)

Below: An unusual image of a tea garden depicting cakes piled high on a table. This image at the Two Brewers Tavern and Tea Garden may show a private party.

Did you know?

What did they Eat?

There is little information on the refreshment offerings of the smaller tea houses and so the plea from the proprietress of the tiny Corney's Tea Gardens in Bedfordshire for her correspondent Mr Dench (the blacksmith in Polegate near Arundel), to 'send two more bushels of quinces' is even more intriguing. Did the Toddington tea garden perhaps specialise in quince jam on its muffins, or sell the traditional quince cheeses? And why all the way from Arundel? Two bushels would, incidentally, be the entire crop of a small quince tree.

Visitors to today's tea gardens may expect something a little more special, as at the Manor House in Stevington. (Courtesy of Kathy Brown)

6
Decline and Resurrection

The outbreak of the Second World War in 1939 was a temporary death knell for the tea garden. Butter and sugar were rationed from January 1940, with rations on tea, milk and jam following in July of that year. Before the war many of the tea gardens that had served food to accompany the inevitable 'tea' would have relied on homegrown and homemade produce and could have continued to produce eggs and even perhaps milk or a low-sugar hedgerow jam, but the essential tea was the problem. With a ration of only 2 ounces of tea per person, there was none available for the enterprising cottager to share with prospective tea garden customers. With no way around the necessity of importation, tea was not to come off rationing until 1952, although the ration per person had been raised to 3 ounces a week some time before that. Flour and bread were also rationed between 1946 and 1948, lengthening the post-war impact for those gardens that had offered additions to the basic teapot refreshment. While licensed restaurants and cafeteria had special allocations, and workers were encouraged to eke out their own rations by eating at one of the British Restaurants set up by the government, the small informal tea garden had no such privileges. Petrol shortages also prevented outings to the countryside that had been so popular in the 1930s. Petrol was the first item to be rationed

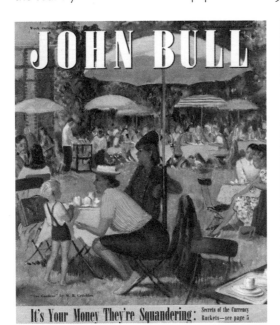 

Above left: In the aftermath of the Second World War, tea gardens offered an air of normality and a reminiscence of peaceful times, although rationing still restricted smaller gardens. (Front cover of *John Bull*, July 1948 (colour litho), English School, Private Collection, © The Advertising Archives/Bridgeman Images)
Above right: Rationing was the death knell for many small tea gardens that did not have a licence.

in 1939, and in 1942 petrol for private use was withdrawn completely, with a permit system ensuring that what little petrol there was was used for essential work only. Many people simply packed their cars away for the duration of the war and the larger charabancs and coaches that had taken people on Sunday outings were commandeered as ambulances or for other war-related purposes. Petrol for private use became available again in 1945, although it was still rationed until 1950. Cycling out into the countryside was, of course, still an ideal way to get away from it all, but with increased workloads and workers being urged to spend any free time in the summer 'lending a hand on the land', the delights of the tea garden would have been a guilty pleasure. The wireless and the cinema, both mixing pleasure with wartime information, were the popular pastimes of the day rather than the great outdoors.

Due to its previous lack of popularity in Britain coffee was never rationed here, and it gradually gained in popularity, being served alongside tea in the famous Lyons Corner Houses and teashops. When American soldiers arrived in Britain they were delighted to find the national beverage on tap.

Did you know?

Two Nations Divided by Drink
During the Second World War tea was rationed in Britain from 1940 until 1952, but due to lack of demand was never restricted in America, while coffee was rationed from 1942 in America to less than half the normal consumption per person, but was 'off ration' in Britain.

S. H. LUPTON, PRINTER & STATIONER, HARROGATE.

THE

TEA HOUSE,

Valley Gardens.

Open from 8 a.m. to 8 p.m.

AFTERNOON TEAS.   ICES.

The Band plays 3-30 to 5.

Lessees:

C. E. Taylor & Co., Ltd.,

THE KIOSK CAFÉ,

16 Parliament Street.

Coffee Roasted Daily.

An early reference to the serving of coffee at a tea garden, here at the large public gardens in Harrogate. (Author's collection)

Before the war, Americans drank about 20 lbs of coffee each per year, but supplies had been restricted in the USA and civilians were urged to drink less to ensure the military got their full supply. With a reputation for fast times and low living, the American-influenced coffee bar spread quickly through London in the post-war years, largely attracting the younger generation, and by the mid-1950s the tea garden was having to compete again with its oldest rival – the coffee house, now reborn as the café. With coffee also widely available at Wimpy Bars (established in 1954) and Golden Eggs (1960s), the instant cup of coffee began to rival the pre-teabag cuppa, at least for the baby boomer generation. Although not directly competing for customers of the more traditional, rural tea garden, cafés became widespread, often replacing neglected teashops and occasionally venturing into the countryside. In fact, images of these few rural cafés suggest that little had changed other than the name, with the same lawns and seating, but the idea of the gentle tea garden with its complex arrangements of kettles, teapots and strainers was lost in a whirl of instant granules. One of the earliest rural cafés was the Salmon's Leap Café and Guest House, Dart Bridge, Buckfastleigh, catering to holidaymakers on Dartmoor as they returned to their pre-war haunts.

As people gradually returned to the delights of the countryside, rural tea gardens also made a comeback alongside the newer 'layby' cafés and tea stops for car drivers. Plastic chairs and matching tables were replete with newly fashionable matching parasols emblazoned with advertising and boasting the delights of Wall's ice cream and Coca-Cola courtesy of the increased prevalence of freezers. The blocks of creamy yellow Wall's ice cream in particular became a popular adjunct to the 1960s and '70s childhood. Colourful annual planting often replaced the traditional orchard and gentle rose arches.

The oddly named Monks' Rest Tea Gardens were typical of post-war tea gardens that were most easily reached by car.

Monks' Rest Tea Gardens, Worlebury, Weston-super-Mare

Above: Wall's Ice Cream provided signs at cafés and tea gardens where their products were sold, as here at The Tea Gardens in Bosherston, c. 1959. (Francis Frith Collection)

Below: Orange was the fashionable colour for parasols in the 1970s.

Brightly coloured bedding at the Old Vicarage Tea Gardens contrasted with the more subtle landscape beyond, as highlighted by the use of colour cards from the 1960s onwards.

Competition was quick to come in the form of the in-house tea room or coffee shop. Taking on a slew of new properties in the post-war period thanks to the National Land Fund, the National Trust raised its membership to a quarter of a million by 1970 and doubled that again in the following five years, and again (to a million) by 1981. With the founding of the National Trust Enterprises (in 1970) came the impetus to provide more facilities for the visiting members and from a small start with homemade cakes provided by volunteers, by 2015 there were over 200 National Trust cafés and tea rooms in its properties, many set within stunning gardens. English Heritage soon followed with cafés and restaurants at first set inside the ticketed area and then moved out to catch passing trade and cater for visitors who want to admire a distant view of a castle without having to actually pay to examine it in detail. However, despite the plethora of attractions with their own cafés and tea rooms, independent tea gardens and tea rooms are now making a comeback, replete with mismatched china, hand-painted and wooden signs, triple-tiered homemade flower cakes, and, of course, bunting. As cycling and walking become more fashionable with the move to healthy living and holidaying at home, the tea garden evokes a nostalgia for the England of the past as well as the chance of a tasty scone or even a gluten-free avocado and chocolate cake! The National Gardens Scheme with its ever-changing array of local gardens to visit encourages garden owners to provide tea and cakes, while the opportunity to make some extra money for charity has encouraged Women's Institutes and other village organisations to open 'pop-up' tea gardens on Sunday afternoons in June and July to catch passing cyclists. Some of these use the village hall but many spread out onto adjoining lawns with tea and cakes made by local villagers in their own kitchens and served on an array of tables and chairs pressed into service from other duties and made at home among lawns and fruit trees in the best tradition of the British tea garden.

S. F. 47. Tea House and Entrance,
Japanese Tea Garden, Golden
Gate Park, San Francisco,
California.

American tea gardens evolved very differently to British, emphasising the Japanese ancestry to tea-drinking and recreating the full Japanese tea garden experience.

Did you know?

While the history and style of the tea garden in England can be traced from the seventeenth-century 'pleasure gardens', those in America appear to have taken their inspiration direct from the Orient. The Japanese Tea Garden at Brackenridge Park, San Antonio (Texas), was created in 1918/19 in an abandoned limestone rock quarry. Prison labour was used to fashion pools, bridges and a 'Japanese' Pagoda, and in 1919 a Mexican-born artist created a replica Japanese Torii gate at the entrance. Sadly, the resident Japanese family who had served refreshments and tended the gardens were evicted in 1941, and the site was renamed the Chinese Tea garden.

7
WHAT NOW?

VISIT A TEA GARDEN

After reading about tea gardens, what could be more appropriate than visiting one! Despite a decline in the late twentieth century, tea gardens are now on the increase again, with many historic tea gardens being re-opened and others newly created, usually in the traditional rustic style. Here are ten of the best to visit:

Note: No opening times are given here as changing seasons and the vagaries of the British weather mean that a typical tea garden will vary in its opening hours almost daily. Many are also on a small scale and may change hands or sadly close down, so do check before setting off with a particular tea garden in mind.

Beanstalk Tea Garden, near Firle, East Sussex
Tel: 01273 858906
Website: www.facebook.com/BeanstalkTeaGarden/
A truly delightful flower-filled small rural tea garden and rooms set in the heart of the Sussex countryside at the foot of the South Downs. Superb cakes and afternoon teas as well as special evening events. Romantic atmosphere with delicate china and a vintage caravan.

Bosh Tea Rooms (was Ye Olde Worlde Tea Garden and Café), Bosherston Village, Pembrokeshire, SA71 5DN
Tel: 01646 661216
Website: www.facebook.com/boshtearooms
Set up in 1921 by Caesar and Sarah Jane Evans, their daughter 'Aunt Vi' (Violet Alice Susannah Evans) lived and worked there for over seventy years. The tea gardens have been renamed but are at the same venue, with the same delightful ivy-clad cottage and the same high standards.

Carnewas Tea Rooms and Tea Garden, near Trenance, Cornwall, PL27 7UW
Tel: 01637 860701
Website: www.carnewas-tea-rooms.co.uk
This café started life as a stable for mining ponies, with the adjoining gardens as a paddock. It has been run for thirty years by the same family and has a reputation for high-quality local produce including Cornish clotted cream. With stunning views over the Bedruthan Steps, wear a windproof if sitting in the gardens of this Cornish cliff-side setting!

Cosy Nook Tea Gardens and Art Gallery, Crantock, Cornwall
Tel: 01637 830324
Tea garden with art gallery situated at the heart of this Cornish village. Serves lunches as well as tea and has won awards for its cream teas.

Pavilions and tents keep off the British rain so you can enjoy a traditional tea garden whatever the weather or the occasion. (Courtesy of Beanstalk Tea Garden, Lewes)

Above: Beanstalk Tea Gardens are everything a traditional tea garden should be – small, quirky, and serving delicious homemade teas and cakes. (Courtesy of Beanstalk Tea Garden)

Below: One of the surviving historic tea gardens, Ye Olde Worlde Café is now known as Bosh Tea Gardens.

Dalehead Farm Tea Garden, Rosedale East, Pickering, North Yorkshire, YO18 8RL
Tel: 01751 417 353
Website: www.daleheadfarmteagarden.co.uk
Based on a working farm, this is an ideal tea garden for those intent on a good cuppa before or after exploring the nearby North Yorkshire Moors. Redolent of so many tea gardens set up to serve the hikers and cyclists of bygone ages, the owner, Maggie, makes traditional cakes and biscuits such as 'Courting Cake' and 'Ginger Moggy', as well as serving tea to thirsty hikers.

Elstow Tea Garden, 209 Church End, Elstow, Bedford, MK42 9XT
Tel: 01234 926677
Website: www.elstowteagarden.weebly.com
A newly established tea garden (since 2011) that is perhaps as close to the original ideal of the small cottage tea garden as you can get. Created in a small garden with catering in a wooden summerhouse, small tables and garden chairs are scattered around a lawn edged with flowerbeds and views of the nearby Elstow Abbey. Knickerbocker Glory, cream tea and toasted teacakes (and of course tea) keep up the traditional theme. The village of Elstow is the birthplace of John Bunyan and many of his followers visit to follow the Bunyan Trail. Limited opening hours.

Follow the signs to a tea garden. (Courtesy of Falling Foss Tea Garden)

Falling Foss Tea Gardens, Midge Hall, Sneaton Forest, Whitby, YO22 5JD
Tel: 07723 477929
Website: www.fallingfossteagarden.co.uk
A tea garden in a magical setting. The fairy-tale cottage of Midge Hall nestles in the woodland at the top of magnificent Falling Foss waterfall, a unique location and a much loved beauty spot. Originally built as a gamekeeper's cottage in the late 1780s, it was used by the gamekeeper's wife to serve teas in the garden well into the 1960s. Having been derelict for almost fifty years, it was restored and re-opened as a tea garden in 2008.

High Park Farm Tea Garden, Little Langdale, Ambleside, Cumbria, LA22 9NS
Tel: 01539 437718
Website: www.cumbriawaybb.co.uk
A stunning location along the Cumbria Way for this recently established and immaculate tea garden. They boast that there are even views from the loo! The best of traditional tea garden small-scale style.

Jane's Enchanted Tea Garden, Mill Lane, Kirtlington, Oxfordshire, OX5 3HW
Website: www.janes-cream-teas.moonfruit.com
Email: themagicteagarden@gmail.com
Developed over the last twenty years, this tea garden combines tradition with flamboyant style and exquisitely decorated cakes. Elderflower, gooseberry, roses, cherries and other delights feature alongside buttermilk scones, with much of the food grown in the garden or nearby smallholding and milk coming from their own Jersey cows. There is no access by car and visitors arrive on foot or by boat along the South Oxford Canal. Booking is absolutely essential!

Kathy Brown's Garden, Manor House, Church Road, Stevington, MK43 7QB
Tel: 01234 822064
Website: www.kathybrownsgarden.homestead.com
Primarily a superbly designed garden, Kathy's dedication to producing superb cakes using a range of specially grown edible flowers from the garden makes her regular afternoon tea openings unique, along with her very special 'Vintage Teas'.

Litlington Tea Gardens, The Street, Litlington, Sussex, BN26 5RB
Tel: 0132 870222
Website: www.bestofengland.com/cafes/litlington-tea-gardens
Established over 150 years ago, Litlington Tea Gardens are set in the unspoilt Cuckmere Valley in Sussex. The tea gardens still retain their quaint Victorian elegance and offer visitors the chance to relax and enjoy morning coffee and light lunches as well as traditional cream tea with homemade cake. Tables are surrounded by a delightful display of shrubs and mature trees while small wooden pavilions provide shelter in the old style.

Orchard Tea Garden, 45–47 Mill Way, Grantchester, Cambridge, CB3 9ND
Tel: 01223 551125
Website: www.theorchardteagarden.co.uk
The most iconic English tea garden forever associated with the Great War poet Rupert Brooke (1887–1915). In 1897 a group of Cambridge students asked Mrs Stevenson of Orchard House if she would serve them tea beneath the blossoming fruit trees rather than, as was usual, on the front lawn of the house and thus started a great Cambridge tradition. The Orchard Tea Garden soon became a popular 'up-river resort', to which students would punt along the river or cycle up the towpaths. Re-opening has seen locals and tourists flock to the gardens, with their ancient pear and apple trees and deckchairs dotted around. There is a small museum dedicated to the life of Rupert Brooke.

Relaxing on a sunny afternoon among the ancient orchard at Grantchester tea garden. (Courtesy of The Orchard Tea Garden, Grantchester)

This is the original Pavilion built around the end of the 19th century in which Brooke, Russell, Forster, Keynes, Virginia Woolf and others took tea when it rained.

The original pavilion still survives at The Orchard Tea Garden in Grantchester. (Courtesy of The Orchard Tea Garden)

Pretty Corner Café and Tea Rooms, Upper Sheringham, Norfolk, NR26 8TW
Tel: 01263 822766
Website: www.prettycornerteagardens.com
Pretty Corner Café and Tea Gardens was first established in 1926 as a small wooden pavilion catering for visitors to this popular part of the Norfolk coast. It is now a delightful café and attractive tea garden that continues to welcome walkers, cyclists, motorists, children and dogs.

DO SOME RESEARCH
Tea gardens are a much neglected part of our social history and in the few places where some historic research has been undertaken the number of gardens uncovered has been astounding.

At Lee in Devon, for example, a short study of the refreshment history of this popular but relatively small village uncovered seventeen tea houses, tea gardens and other various tea-serving establishments! The seventeen included three traditional tea gardens, a converted cow shed-cum-tea garden, a hotel, a beachside tea house, tea cottages that may or may not have catered on the premises, as well as serving take-away tea, a post office-cum-tea house, and a mobile home tea house that has twice been blown away by sea gales. From the 1880s to the present day, one has never been short of a cup of tea in Lee.

With the simple aids of old maps, a hunt for old postcards, a look through Kelly's Directories of establishments in the nineteenth and twentieth centuries, and a chat to local people, the number and history of tea houses and tea gardens known in any locality can be revealed. With

Is this the proprietor of Ye Olde Two Brewers, or an enthusiastic customer? Note the rustic chairs and arch in true tea gardens style. (Courtesy of Anne Andrews, Dorset Gardens Trust)

Above: A surviving photograph of Ye Olde Two Brewers Tavern and Tea Garden may encourage researchers to find out more. (Courtesy of Anne Andrews, Dorset Gardens Trust)
Below: More typical offerings can just be glimpsed on the smaller side plates at one of the numerous tea gardens at Lee, Sussex. (Author's collection)

more research will come better understanding of these evocative and attractive elements of our social and garden history, as well as finding out more about the people who owned them and visited them.

Get started by looking on eBay for postcards and memorabilia of tea gardens close to you, or visit your local county archives to find out more. Your local county Gardens Trust may also be able to help, or welcome your assistance.

READ MORE ABOUT TEA AND TEA ROOMS

In between consuming tea and scones you can read more about the subject of tea, teapots, tea gardens and also spa gardens in these books:

Curl, James Steven, *Spas, Wells & Pleasure Gardens of London* (London: Historical Publications Ltd, 2010). *A wonderful insight into the pastimes and gardens of old London.*

Downing, Sarah Jane, *The English Pleasure Garden 1660–1860* (Oxford: Shire Publications, 2011). *Concise and wonderfully illustrated history of pleasure and spa gardens of all kinds.*

Emmerson, Robin, *British Teapots & Tea Drinking, 1700–1850* (London: HMSO, 1992). *Ideal for those that seriously want to know more about the tea they are drinking and the history of pots and tea accessories.*

Hembry, Phyllis May, *The English Spa, 1560–1815 A Social History* (London: Athlone Press, 1990).

Hohenegger, Beatrice *Steeped in History: The Art of Tea* (Los Angeles: UCLA, 2009). *Images to thrill the heart of every tea drinker.*

Masset, Claire, *Tea and Tea Drinking* (Oxford: Shire Publications, 2012). *A super, well illustrated and short book on one of the most enjoyable of activities.*